Living Things

Module A

Living Things

How can an animal be like a plant? Animals and plants look different. But animals and plants are alike in an important way. They are living things.

Chapter 1

Plants and Animals

It can be fun to learn about different kinds of animals and plants! How do animals and plants get the things they need to stay alive? Page **A 4**

Chapter 2

Where Things Live

Each animal and plant lives in its own special place. Where do some animals and plants you know about live? Page **A 24**

Chapter 3

Grouping Living Things

You can sort objects into groups by color or shape or size. Can you sort animals and plants into groups too?

Page **A 42**

Chapter 1

Plants and Animals

Did you ever wish that you could be a different animal for a day? You might like to be a bird. What kind of bird would you be?

How would you look if you were a bird? You might have bright blue feathers. Or you could have webbed feet.

What other special body parts might you have? What things could you do that you can't do now?

What body parts do animals have?

1. Find a picture of an animal in a book.
2. Look at the animal in your picture. Tell what you see.
3. Draw what you see.
4. **Tell about it.** Tell how you and the animal are alike. Tell how you and the animal are different.

Ask me what else I want to find out about animals.

How do body parts help animals live?

You just found out that animals have many kinds of body parts. These body parts can help animals stay alive. Here is how body parts help a butterfly stay alive.

Look at the big wings of this butterfly. Wings help it fly to flowers. Flowers hold a sweet food called nectar. Some butterflies eat nectar.

The butterfly has two large eyes and two long antennas. The eyes help the butterfly see flowers. The antennas help the butterfly touch and smell the flowers.

The butterfly has six legs. It uses its legs to hold onto the flower. The butterfly has a mouth like a long tube. It uses its mouth to sip nectar from a flower.

wings

antennas

eyes

mouth

body

legs

Checkpoint

Tell a story about how a butterfly uses its body parts to live.

What actions help animals stay alive?

What do animals do when they hear a noise? A bird may fly away. A squirrel may run and hide.

Animals have ways of acting that help them stay alive. A noise may be a sign of danger. Running away may help an animal get away from danger. The pictures tell about other ways that animals act.

A muskrat builds its home in a pond. Other animals cannot reach it.

A squirrel buries acorns. Later it digs them up and eats them.

Checkpoint

Tell about a way of acting that helps an animal.

A duck hides her eggs from other animals.

A woodchuck **hibernates** in winter. It hardly moves. It needs very little food.

How can color make things hard to see?

Could a bird see a brown caterpillar crawling on a brown twig? You can find out how color can make things hard to see.

You will need:

○ white paper circles

● brown paper circles

 brown paper

 timer

Find out about it.

1. Get 20 white circles and 20 brown circles.

2. Have your partner place all the circles on brown paper.

3. Have your partner start the timer.

4. Use one hand. Pick up as many circles as you can in 10 seconds. Pick up one circle at a time.

5. Count the white circles you picked up. Count the brown circles you picked up.

Write about it.

Make a chart like this. Write the number of circles you picked up.

colors	circles picked up
white	
brown	

Checkpoint

1. Which color was harder to find?

2. **Take Action!** Draw a picture of an animal. Use color to make the animal hard to see.

How do color and shape help animals?

Think about a green caterpillar on a green leaf. Its color matches the place where it lives. Its color makes the caterpillar hard to see.

A color or shape that makes an animal hard to see is **camouflage.** Camouflage can hide an animal from other animals that might eat it. Find the animals in the pictures. How does camouflage hide each animal?

Checkpoint

Write a story about how camouflage helps animals.

deer

walking stick

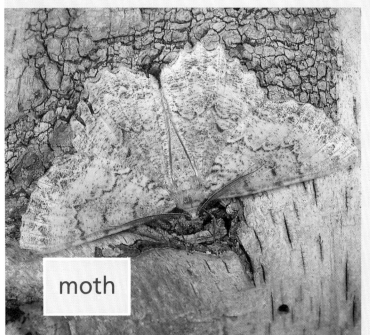

moth

hornworm

tree frogs

What parts help plants live?

Pretend you are walking on this city sidewalk. You notice trees and other plants. Plants have roots that grow under the ground. The roots help hold plants in the soil.

Roots take in water from the soil. Plants need water to live. Roots help keep trees and other plants alive.

Find the trunk of this tree. It holds up the heavy branches. The trunk is a thick stem. Stems carry water from the roots to other parts of plants.

Now find the leaves on the tree. Leaves use sunlight to help make food for plants.

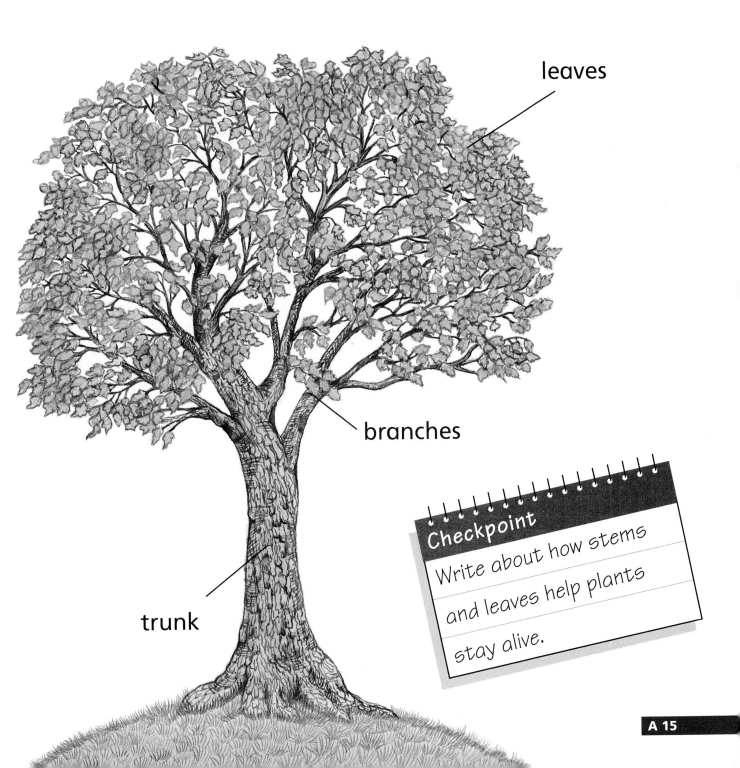

leaves

branches

trunk

Checkpoint

Write about how stems and leaves help plants stay alive.

How do some plants store water?

Suppose you live in a place that gets very little rain. You might see a cactus growing in such a dry place.

Look at the thick stems of a cactus. The stems hold water for a long time. The stored water helps the cactus grow in the desert.

Other plants store water in their leaves. Now let's see how thick leaves hold water.

Observe how plants store water.

You will need: potted jade plant

 potted fern plant  water

1. Place the plants next to each other.
2. Water each plant. Make sure each plant gets the same amount of water.
3. Do not water either plant again.
4. Watch the plants until you see a change.
5. Touch the leaves carefully. Look for changes in the leaves.

Checkpoint

Tell how you know which plant stored more water. Which plant would grow better in a dry place?

What helps plants grow in new places?

Do you ever blow on a dandelion? You may like watching the dandelion fruits float through the air. When fruits float through the air, the seeds inside are scattered. Scattering helps carry the seeds to new places where they can grow. You can show how seeds are scattered through the air.

Show how seeds are scattered.

You will need: cotton balls construction paper

1. Place the paper on the floor.
2. Pull a small piece from a cotton ball.
3. Stand over the paper. Hold your arm out straight from your shoulder. Drop the cotton piece.
4. Do this ten times.
5. Watch where the pieces of cotton fall.

Checkpoint

Tell where the pieces of cotton fell. How are the pieces of cotton like dandelion seeds?

How are seeds scattered?

Many seeds are inside fruits. Some fruits have parts like wings or hooks. Wings help seeds be scattered by wind. Hooks help seeds be scattered by animals. The hooks can stick to animal fur. When the animal moves the fruits and seeds are carried to new places.

1. Fruit A has a part like a wing. It might be scattered by wind. Fruit B has hooks. It might be scattered by animals. Look at the other fruits. How might the parts help the seeds be scattered?

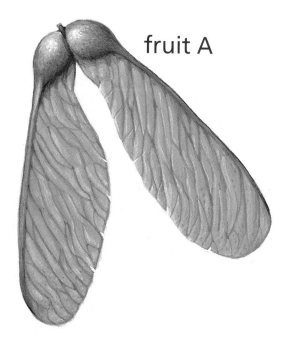
fruit A

fruit B

2. Make a chart like this one.

fruit	how it looks	wings or hooks	how scattered
fruit A	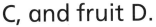	wings	wind
fruit B			
fruit C			
fruit D			

3. The chart shows fruit A. It shows its parts. It shows how the fruits and seeds are scattered. Fill in the chart for fruit B, fruit C, and fruit D.

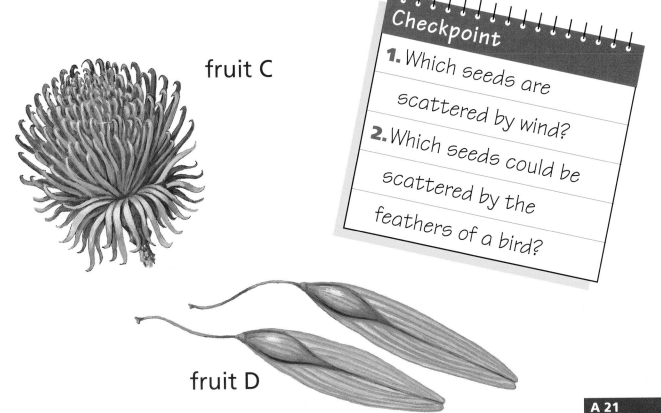

fruit C

fruit D

Checkpoint
1. Which seeds are scattered by wind?
2. Which seeds could be scattered by the feathers of a bird?

What did you learn?

Now you know that body parts and ways of acting help animals stay alive. You also know that special parts help plants grow. You can pretend you are a plant or an animal. Then you can play a game.

You will need: ☐ paper ✏ pencil

Play a guessing game.

1. Work with a group. Make a list of plants and animals.
2. Decide who will take the part of each plant and each animal.
3. Write the name of the plant or animal on a piece of paper.
4. Write down what parts or ways of acting help your plant or animal stay alive.
5. Act out the part of your plant or animal.
6. Ask the class to guess your plant or animal.

Share what you learned.

1. How did you guess what your classmates were pretending to be?
2. What was your favorite animal in the game?

Chapter 2

Where Things Live

Pretend you have a pen pal. You want to tell your pen pal about your home. What can you tell about the place where you live?

You might want to write about your neighborhood too. What can you tell about it? You can tell how it looks. You can tell about the plants and animals that live there. What kinds of places do plants and animals live in? Let's take a look!

Where do you see plants and animals?

1. Cut out pictures of places where plants and animals live.

2. Glue each picture on a paper.

3. Write the names of plants and animals that live in each place.

4. **Tell about it.** Write a story about one kind of place where plants and animals live.

Ask me what else I want to find out about where plants and animals live.

Where do plants and animals live?

The place where a plant or animal lives is a **habitat.** Different plants and animals live in different kinds of habitats.

What can you tell about a habitat? You can tell how a habitat looks. You can tell how warm or cold it is. Think about other things to tell about a habitat. Then tell about the habitat in the picture.

Make a habitat for a plant.

You will need: paper cup stones plant water 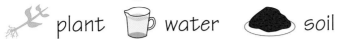 soil

1. Put stones in the bottom of your cup. Add soil to your cup.
2. Put your plant in the cup. Cover the roots with soil.
3. Add water to the cup.
4. Put your plant in a sunny place.

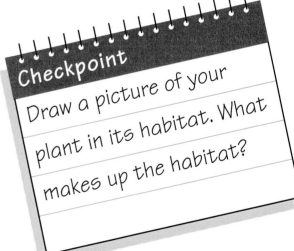

Checkpoint

Draw a picture of your plant in its habitat. What makes up the habitat?

What lives in a water habitat?

It is time for a habitat adventure. You can find out about a water habitat. Get ready to explore the pond in the picture!

You row your boat across the water. You look around. What plants do you see? What animals do you see? What can you tell about the habitat of each plant and animal?

Checkpoint

Pretend you are a plant or animal that lives in a water habitat. Tell about the habitat.

water strider

duck

dragonfly

pond habitat

turtle

How does a habitat help living things?

What do plants and animals get from their habitats? They get everything they need to live. Animals get food and water from their habitats. This spider catches insects in a web. The spider gets food and water from eating the insects.

Animals get the air they need from their habitats. They get a place to live. Animals may also get shelter to protect them from weather or danger.

What else do you see in this garden? You can see that plants live in the garden too.

The plants get sunlight. Plants get water from the soil. They get air. Plants use water, sunlight, and air to make the food they need. The garden habitat has everything the plants need to live.

Checkpoint

Tell a story about a plant or animal that lives in a garden. Tell what the plant or animal gets from its habitat.

How can you make a habitat?

Crickets and other animals need food and water. What else do crickets need to live? How can you make a habitat for crickets?

You will need:

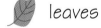 large box

 leaves

 soil

 food

 sticks

 2 crickets

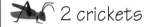 dropper of water

 jar lid

Find out about it.

1 Put soil in the bottom of the box.

2 Add the sticks and leaves to the box. The crickets use sticks and leaves for shelter.

3 Put the food in the box. Put water in the jar lid. Put the lid in the box.

4 Put the crickets in the box.

5 Observe the crickets.

Write about it.

Make a chart like this. Write or draw what you found out about a habitat for crickets.

what crickets need	what habitat has
food	
water	
shelter	

Checkpoint

1. What did the crickets get from the habitat you made?

2. Take Action! Draw a picture of the crickets in the habitat you made.

What habitats are in a zoo?

You see monkeys swinging from trees. You watch seals splashing in water. Where are you? You are visiting the zoo.

Many animals live at the zoo. People who work at the zoo give food and water to the animals. Look at the zoo habitats of these animals. Each animal gets everything it needs from its zoo habitat.

Checkpoint

Draw or paint a picture that shows an animal in a zoo habitat.

monkey

tiger

panda

giraffe

What habitat can you plan for a zoo?

Look in this tree. Tell about the animal you see. It is a koala. The tree is its habitat. How does this koala get everything it needs?

The koala gets food and water from eating leaves. It gets shelter from the tree.

Pretend you work in a zoo. Your job is to make a habitat for a koala.

Make a model of a zoo habitat.

You will need: cover goggles shoe box

 construction paper crayons glue

 scissors pipe cleaners

1. Draw a picture of a koala. Cut out your picture.
2. Make a habitat for the koala in your shoe box.
3. Put your koala in its habitat.

Checkpoint

Do a radio show. Tell about the new zoo habitat for the koala. Invite people to come to the zoo.

How many red wolves live in wildlife parks?

Sometimes red wolves cannot live in their habitat. Some of these red wolves are sent to live in wildlife parks. These habitats have everything the red wolves need to live.

1. Look at the pictures. You can see that 20 red wolves were sent to habitat A. How many wolves went to each of the other habitats?

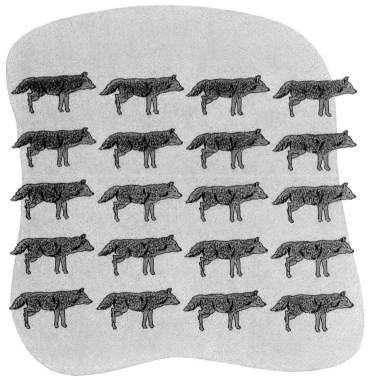

habitat A

habitat B

2. Draw a chart like this one.

habitat	number of wolves
habitat A	20
habitat B	
habitat C	

3. The chart shows how many red wolves live in habitat A. Fill in the chart for habitats B and C.

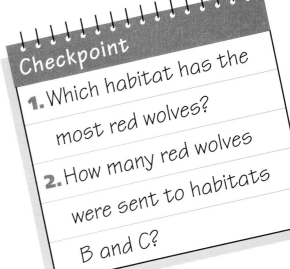

Checkpoint

1. Which habitat has the most red wolves?

2. How many red wolves were sent to habitats B and C?

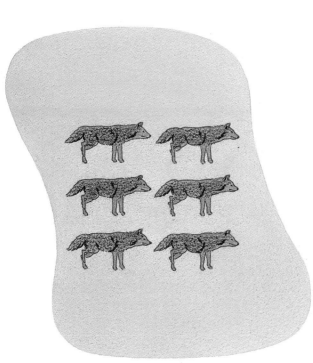

habitat C

What did you learn?

You learned what plants and animals get from their habitats. Now make a habitat book. Show a habitat for a plant or animal. Then tell about the habitat.

You will need: crayons paper  pencil

Make a book about a habitat.

1. Draw a picture of a plant or animal on your paper.
2. Add a habitat for the plant or animal to your picture.
3. Write a story on another paper. Tell what the plant or animal needs to live.
4. Make a cover for your book.
5. Put the pages inside the cover.

A 41

Chapter 3

Grouping Living Things

Look at all these shoes! Do any of them look like yours? Do any of them look alike? Things that are alike can be grouped together.

Now look around your classroom. Find more shoes. How could you group these shoes?

How can you group things?

1 Draw your favorite shoe.

2 Color the shoe. Then cut it out.

3 Sit in a circle with your classmates. Put your shoe picture in the center of the circle.

4 Find the shoes that are the same color. Put them in a group.

5 Group the shoes in as many other ways as you can.

6 **Tell about it.** Write down how the shoes in each group are alike.

Ask me what else I want to find out about grouping things.

Is it living?

Pretend you are taking a walk. You might see a bird. You might see grass. How are the bird and the grass alike? They are **living things.** Living things can grow.

What other things do you see? You might see a building. You might see a rock. Buildings and rocks are **nonliving things.** They do not grow. What other nonliving things might you see?

Group living and nonliving things.

You will need: magazines ✂ scissors

1. Look at the pictures in the magazines.
2. Cut out pictures of living things. Cut out pictures of nonliving things.
3. Put pictures of living things in a group. Put pictures of nonliving things in a group.

Checkpoint
Tell a story about one of your pictures.

How are living things grouped?

Pretend you are visiting a park. You see living things in the park. How can you group these living things?

You can put the chipmunk, bird, and the ladybug into one group. How are they alike? They are animals. Most animals can move from place to place. Animals eat the food they find in their habitats.

You can put the grass and the trees into another group. How are grass and trees alike? They are plants. Plants cannot move from one place to another. Plants use sunlight to make the food they need.

Checkpoint

Write a commercial for a new park. Tell what groups of living things people can see in the park.

What are some groups of animals?

Imagine walking into this pet store. There are so many animals to see!

First find the animals that live in water. Did you find the fish? Now look for the birds. How are they alike? Notice that animals that are alike are grouped together. Find other groups of animals in the picture.

Checkpoint

Draw a picture of an animal. Write the name of the group the animal belongs to.

Canaries belong to a group called **birds.**

Turtles belong to a group called **reptiles.**

CHEWING TOYS

Goldfish belong to a group called **fish.**

Frogs belong to a group called **amphibians.**

Cats belong to a group called **mammals.**

What are some kinds of body coverings?

Imagine petting this soft, furry puppy. A puppy is a mammal. Mammals have hair or fur covering their bodies. Do other kinds of animals feel furry? Reptiles have rough, dry skin. Amphibians have smooth, wet skin.

Birds have feathers covering their bodies. Most fish have scales covering their bodies. What are feathers and scales like?

Observe body coverings.

You will need:  bird feather ○ hand lens

fish scales ☐ paper pencil

1. Look at the feather with the hand lens. Draw what you see.
2. Touch the feather. Feel the different parts. Write down how the feather feels.
3. Look at the fish scales with the hand lens. Draw what you see.
4. Touch the fish scales. Write down how the scales feel.

Checkpoint

Write a story about an animal. Tell about its body covering.

What are some other groups of animals?

Pretend you are digging in this soil. You find a worm. You look at it. The worm has a long soft body. It does not have legs. You watch the worm crawl around the ground. The worm in this picture lives in soil. Other worms live in water.

You see an ant on a nearby flower. Ants belong to a group of animals called **insects.** Ants and other insects have three main body parts. Insects have six legs. Many ants do not have wings. Insects such as bees do have wings.

You find other animals on the ground. You see a spider. It has two main body parts. You notice that the spider does not have wings. You count eight legs on the spider.

Checkpoint

Draw a picture of a spider. Show the body parts of the spider.

How can you make a model of an insect?

Suppose you see an insect on your way to school. You want to tell a classmate about the insect. One way to tell about the insect is to make a model.

You will need:

 cover goggles

 picture of an insect

 clay

 paper

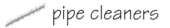 pipe cleaners

 scissors

 glue

Find out about it.

1. Get a picture of an insect from your teacher. Look closely at the picture.

2. Make the main body parts of the insect out of pieces of clay. Use pipe cleaners to put the parts together.

3. Make legs from pipe cleaners.

4. Put the legs on the body of the insect.

5. Add other parts your insect might have.

Write about it.

Make a chart like this one. Write down how many parts your model has.

kind of part	how many parts
main body parts	
legs	
wings	
antennas	
eyes	

Checkpoint

1. What kind of insect did you make?
2. Take Action! Tell how your model is different from a model made by a classmate.

How do you group plants?

Pretend you are looking at plants with flowers. You see veins in the leaves.

The veins of some leaves are in straight lines. The veins of other leaves spread out like a web.

1. Look at the pictures. Leaf A has veins that are spread out. Leaf B has veins that are in straight lines. How do the veins in leaf C and leaf D look?

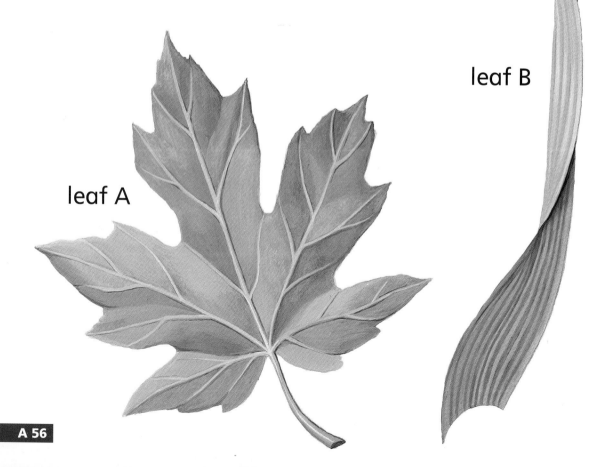

leaf B

leaf A

2. Make a chart like this one.

leaf	how leaf looks	veins in straight lines	veins that spread out
leaf A			X
leaf B		X	
leaf C			
leaf D			

3. The chart tells about the veins in leaf A and leaf B. Fill in the chart for leaf C and leaf D.

leaf C

leaf D

Checkpoint

1. Which leaves have veins in straight lines?

2. Which leaves have veins like webs?

What did you learn?

You can match living and nonliving things with words that tell about them.

You will need: [ ] note cards  pencil

Play a matching game.

1. Get 8 note cards from your teacher.
2. Write 8 things from this list on your note cards.

worm	nonliving
bird	plant
spider	long, soft body
fish	veins
insect	feathers
building	8 legs
tree	scales
leaf	6 legs

3. Tell your partner to write the 8 other things on note cards.

4. Put all the cards face down on the table.
5. Turn one card over.
6. Pick up another card to match the first card. Turn the card face down if it is not a match.
7. Play until a match is made. Keep the matched cards face up on the table.
8. Take turns until all the cards are matched.

Share what you learned.

1. What 2 cards did you match first?
2. What kinds of animals do you see on your way to school? What words tell about the animals?

A visit to a pet store

Imagine visiting a pet store. You see rabbits sleeping. You hear birds singing. You watch fish swimming in aquariums. What else might you see?

Pet store workers take care of the animals. The workers make sure the animals stay healthy. The workers clean the cages. They clean the aquariums. Pet store workers give the animals food and water every day.

How does an aquarium work?

1 The air pump puts air into the water.

2 The filter keeps the water clean.

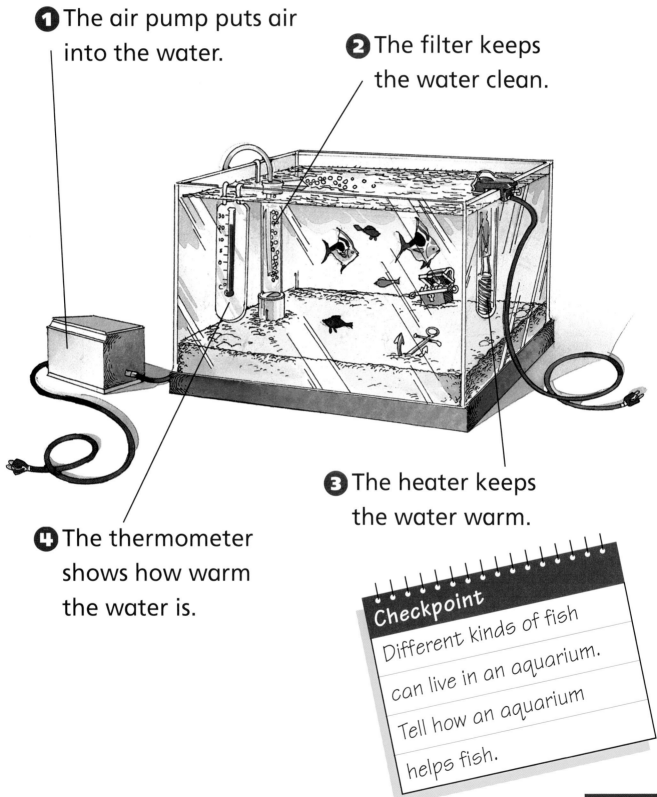

4 The thermometer shows how warm the water is.

3 The heater keeps the water warm.

Checkpoint

Different kinds of fish can live in an aquarium.

Tell how an aquarium helps fish.

Show what you know.

Suppose you want to tell about one animal or plant. You can tell how it looks. You can tell about its habitat. What else can you tell? Choose an animal or plant you want to tell about. Have a nature show to tell others about your plant or animal.

Plan your nature show.

1. Pick a project you would like to do.
2. Get what you need to do your project.
3. What will you do first?
4. Think about how you will tell about your animal or plant.

Make a mobile.

Draw a big picture of your plant or animal. Draw pictures about your plant or animal on note cards. Tape yarn to each card. Tape the cards to the big picture. Hang your mobile!

Put on a play.

Pretend to be an animal or plant. Act out what your animal or plant does. Show other things about your animal or plant. See if your classmates can guess what you are.

Give a report.

Write a report about your animal or plant. Draw pictures that go with your report. Give your report to your class.

Share what you know.

1. Show others what you have done.

2. What did you like the most about the way your project turned out?

Contents

Kids Are for the Birds

Birds don't have an easy life! They need lots of food to live. Our class wanted birds to find enough food in our schoolyard. So we decided to make bird feeders.

We worked in teams. First, we decided what kinds of birds would use our feeders. Next, we learned about the birds. We read about what they eat. We found out whether they need feeders with perches. We found out other things we needed to know.

Then we planned our feeders. They had to be the right size and shape for the birds. They had to hold the right kind of food. We also had to plan how to keep squirrels away.

Next, we made our bird feeders. When we were finished, we got together and shared them. It was fun to learn about different kinds of bird feeders. Finally, we put our bird feeders in different places around our school. Then we all became bird watchers!

You can do it.

Draw a picture of a bird feeder you would like to make. Tell about your bird feeder.

Kids Save the Earth

Our class thinks the earth is a beautiful place! So we think it's important to take care of the earth. We wanted to share ways to help the earth. So our class made up an alphabet game!

First, we each picked a letter of the alphabet. Then we made big paper letters. Next, we thought of a word that starts with our letter.

The word had to tell about a problem on the earth or a way to help the earth. Then we made a drawing about the word on our paper letter.

Finally, we all got together and shared our letters. We learned about ways to solve problems on the earth. Then we put our letters on our bulletin board. We invited other classes to see our ABC's About Our Earth. We were proud of what we had done!

You can do it.

Tell a friend about a problem on the earth. Talk about ways to solve the problem.

Kids Make It Move

Our teacher gave our class a problem to solve. We had to move a marble. The marble was on a table. We had to move the marble to a bowl on the floor. So we invented machines to help us move the marble.

First, each team made a plan for its invention. Next, we collected things we needed to build our machines. We collected cardboard tubes and boxes. We collected straws, paper cups, and many other things.

Then we built our machines and tested them. It was fun to watch how they worked! Finally our teams got together to share our inventions. Our class invented some very strange machines!

You can do it.

Invent a machine to move a marble. Share your invention with your classmates.

Kids Save Soil

Our new schoolyard was a dusty and muddy place to play. The ground was bare in some places. The soil in these places was blowing away. When it rained, the ground got muddy and soil washed away.

Our class wanted to help save the soil. So we made a map of the bare spots of land. Then we made a plan to take care of the bare land.

We found out that the roots of plants hold soil in the ground. Then the soil cannot be blown or washed away. So we decided to plant grass, flowers, and trees.

Each team picked a spot of land to care for. Our teams planted grass seeds and flower seeds. We planted flowers and trees. Soon colorful plants covered the bare ground.

You can do it.

Walk around your school or neighborhood. Find a place where the ground is bare. Tell what you could plant there.

Study Guide

Answer the questions. Use your own paper.

Chapter 1 Plants and Animals

A 4-5 1. Animals have special ____ parts.

        leaf   body   floating

A 6-7 2. Look at the picture. What part does the butterfly use to smell flowers?

        a. _____

        b. _____

        c. _____

A 8-9 3. Animals have ways of acting that help them ____ .

        stay alive   stay cold   stay small

        4. An animal hardly moves when it ____ .

        flies   hibernates   eats

A 10-11 5. A brown caterpillar would be hard to see on a ____ leaf.

        green   yellow   brown

A 12-13 6. A color or shape that makes an animal hard to see is called ____ .

        nectar   red   camouflage

A 14-15 7. Plant ____ take in water from the soil.

        leaves   roots   flowers

8. Look at the picture. Which plant parts make food the plant needs to live?

a. ____

b. ____

c. ____

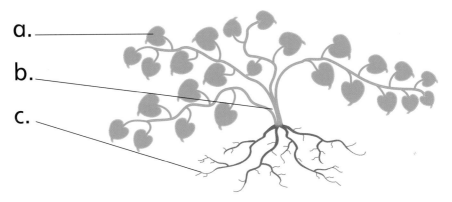

A 16-17 9. The thick ____ of the cactus hold water.

stems   leaves   seeds

A 18-19 10. Dandelion seeds are ____ through the air.

scattered   planted   grown

Chapter 2 Where Things Live

A 24-25 1. Plants and animals have special places where they ____ .

work   live   walk

A 26-27 2. Plants and animals live in many different kinds of ____ .

rocks   sunlight   habitats

A 28-29 3. A pond is one kind of ____ habitat.

dry   water   snowy

4. Green plants, ducks, and ____ might live in a pond habitat.

turtles   elephants   dogs

Study Guide

A 30-31 5. Animals get food, water, and ____ from their habitats.

insects   shelter   fur

6. A habitat gives plants ____ that they need to live.

nothing   some things   everything

A 32-33 7. Look at the pictures. Which of these is a good habitat for a cricket?

a.   b.   c.

A 34-35 8. Zoo habitats are built to give each kind of ____ everything it needs.

cage   animal   tree

A 36-37 9. Which of these is in a habitat for koalas?

a tree   an apple   a pond

Chapter 3 Grouping Living Things

A 42-43 1. You can ____ things by how the things are alike.

smell   group   float

A 44-45 2. A rock is a ____ thing.

living   growing   nonliving

3. Birds and grasses are kinds of ____ .
plants   nonliving things   living things

A 46-47 **4.** Plants use ____ to make food they need.
animals   habitats   sunlight

A 48-49 **5.** A turtle belongs to a group of animals called ____ .
birds   fish   reptiles

6. Look at the pictures. Which animal belongs to a group called amphibians?
a.   b.   c.

A 50-51 **7.** Animals with body hair or fur are ____ .
turtles   mammals   fish

8. Birds have ____ on their bodies.
feathers   scales   fur

A 52-53 **9.** A ____ is an animal with no legs.
spider   worm   bee

10. Spiders have ____ legs.
four   eight   six

11. Insects have ____ main body parts.
three   six   eight

Study Guide

Answer the questions. Use your own paper.

Chapter 1 Discovering Dinosaurs

B 4-5 1. Dinosaurs lived in ____ on the earth.

cities   many places   buildings

B 6-7 2. What size were dinosaurs?

only big   big and small   only small

B 8-9 3. Could some dinosaurs fit in a space the size of your classroom?

never   no   yes

B 10-11 4. Dinosaurs with long sharp teeth ate ____ .

leaves   meat   flowers

5. Look at the pictures. Which kind of food did dinosaurs with big, flat teeth eat?

a.   b.   c.

B 12-13 6. Dinosaur ____ tell how dinosaurs looked or acted.

tails   names   teeth

7. What does the word dinosaur mean?

big animal   terrible lizard   fast runner

B 14-15   **8.** Did all dinosaurs run fast?

     always   yes   no

Chapter 2   Dinosaur Detectives

B 20-21   **1.** Looking at ____ can tell about a person.

     questions   dinosaurs   objects

B 22-23   **2.** Dinosaurs left behind ____ .

     buildings   footprints   mud

B 24-25   **3.** A ____ can be a part or mark from an animal or plant.

     shell   fossil   tool

B 26-27   **4.** Look at the pictures. Which fossil came from a plant?

     a.   b.   c.

B 28-29   **5.** Fossils are ____ rocks and dirt.

     on top of   buried in   never found in

B 30-31   **6.** Some dinosaur bones became ____ .

     mud   rocks   fossils

     7. Dinosaur fossils tell us about ____ .

     dinosaurs   people   plants

Study Guide

B 32-33 **8.** Dinosaur _____ can fit together like puzzle pieces fit together.

footprints   shapes   bones

B 34-35 **9.** Many fossils of dinosaur babies were found in _____ .

trees   nests   lakes

10. People learned about dinosaurs and their babies from studying _____ .

plants   mud   fossils

B 36-37 **11.** Fossils tell us about _____

long ago   people   puzzles

12. Look at the pictures. Which animal lived at the time of the dinosaurs?

a.   b.   c.

Chapter 3 A Changing World

B 42-43 **1.** The world is always _____ .

small   cold   changing

B 44-45 **2.** Kinds of animals are _____ when they no longer live on earth.

extinct   harmed   endangered

3. Which of these may have made dinosaurs become extinct?

fossils　　　　people　　　　cold weather

B 46-47 **4.** Plants and animals may not get what they need when their ____ change.

names　　　　habitats　　　　fossils

5. Kinds of plants and animals may become ____ if they cannot get what they need.

extinct　　　　bigger　　　　polluted

B 48-49 **6.** Kinds of plants and animals are ____ when only a few of them are still living on earth.

extinct　　　　fossils　　　　endangered

B 50-51 **7.** Polluted water is ____ water.

clean　　　　dirty　　　　safe

B 52-53 **8.** Smoke can make air become ____ .

polluted　　　　fresh　　　　clean

B 54-55 **9.** Look at the pictures. Which picture shows a way to help protect animals?

a.　　　　b. 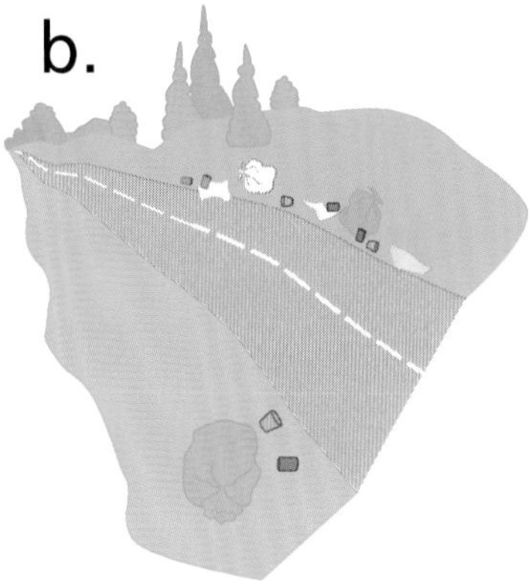　　　　c.

Study Guide

Answer the questions. Use your own paper.

Chapter 1 How Things Move

C 4-5 1. A strong wind can make a sailboat ____ .
stay still   move   float

C 6-7 2. A push or a ____ is a force.
pull   turn   boat

3. You use ____ when you pull an object.
sound   light   force

C 8-9 4. Look at the pictures. Which picture shows a pull?

a.   b.    c.

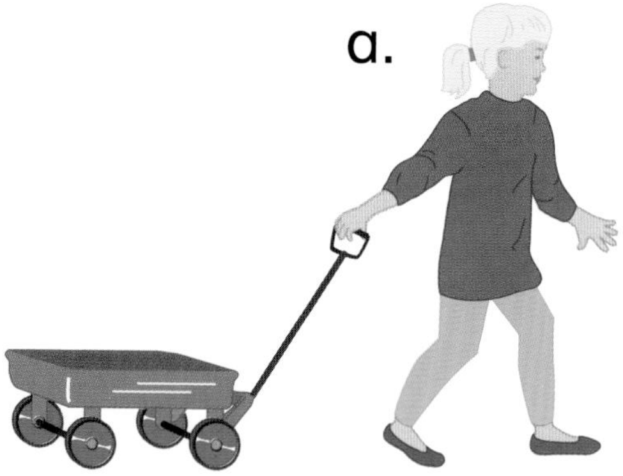

C 10-11 5. Which push will make a ball roll farther?
strong push   weak push   no push

C 12-13 6. Which force will make a rubber band stretch the longest?
no force   weak force   strong force

C 14-15 7. It takes ____ force to move a heavy object than it does to move a light object.
less   more   weaker

8. Look at the pictures. Which pile of books would take the most force to move?

a.   b.   c.

C 16-17 **9.** It is easiest to pull a heavy box over a
_____ surface.

rough   bumpy   smooth

Chapter 2 Magnets

C 22-23 **1.** Two _____ can push and pull each other.
tables   metals   magnets

C 24-25 **2.** The ends of magnets are called north and
south _____ .
poles   pushes   pulls

3. Two north poles held together will _____ .
push apart   pull together   not move

C 26-27 **4.** A magnet will pick up _____ .
a paper clip   an eraser   a paper

5. A magnet will not pick up _____ .
metal   paper clips   plastic

C 28-29 **6.** A _____ might have a magnet.
towel   toy   newspaper

C 30-31 7. A magnet can ____ through paper.

freeze   pull   bounce

C 32-33 8. A weak magnet will pick up ____ paper clips than a strong magnet.

more   heavier   fewer

C 34-35 9. A battery and a wire can turn a nail into a ____ .

magnet   hammer   paper clip

Chapter 3 Moving and Machines

C 40-41 1. You can find ways to move ____ in your classroom more easily.

trees   hammers   objects

C 42-43 2. A ____ makes work easier.

plant   machine   tree

3. Look at the pictures. Which picture shows a machine?

a.   b. 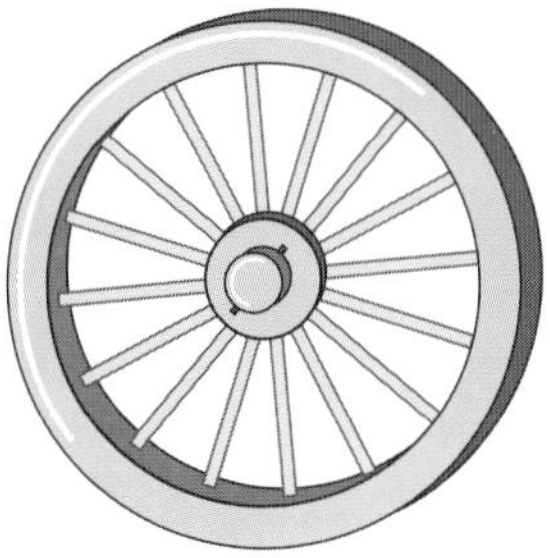   c.

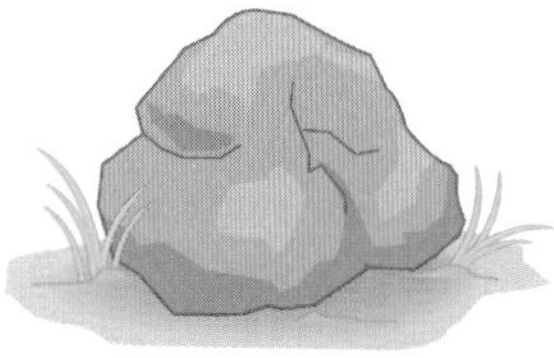

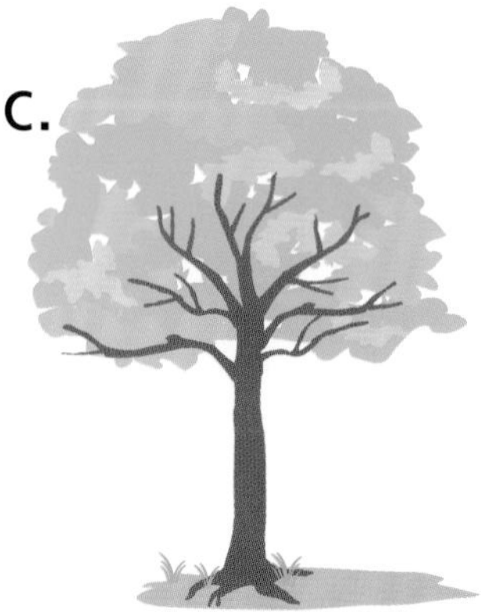

C 44-45 4. A ____ can help you move a wheelchair.

hammer   ramp   skateboard

C 46-47   **5.** A _____ is a lever.

seesaw   wagon   ball bearing

C 48-49   **6.** Ball bearings can make it easier to _____ things.

smell   move   stretch

7. Which of these are like ball bearings?

marbles   blocks   ramps

C 50-51   **8.** When you drink milk, you use your arm like _____ .

a lever   a ramp   a ball bearing

9. Which of these body parts is like a machine?

a.   b.   c.

C 52-53   **10.** Your bones and muscles help you _____ .

learn   move   see

11. _____ in your body help you twist.

Joints   Arms   Bones

C 54-55   **12.** Bones and muscles work _____ .

alone   together   slowly

13. Muscles change _____ when bones move.

size   color   taste

Study Guide

Answer the questions. Use your own paper.

Chapter 1 The Sun

D 4-5 1. Night sky and day sky are ____ .
different   the same   both dark

D 6-7 2. The part of the earth that the sun is shining on has ____ .
nighttime   daytime   rain

D 8-9 3. The ____ is bigger than the earth.
sun   moon   cloud

D 10-11 4. The sun is made of hot ____ .
rocks   water   gases

D 12-13 5. Plants need ____ to grow.
darkness   sunlight   cold air

6. Look at the pictures. Which plant gets the sunlight it needs?
a.   b.   c.

D 14-15 7. Plants that animals eat need ____ to live and grow.
sunlight   clouds   moonlight

D 16-17 8. Energy that comes from the sun is called
_____ energy.

warm   fast   solar

D 18-19 9. Plants and animals that died long ago
changed into coal and _____ .

oil   air   water

Chapter 2 The Moon and Stars

D 24-25 1. Look at the pictures. Which picture shows
things you can see in the night sky?

a.   b.    c.

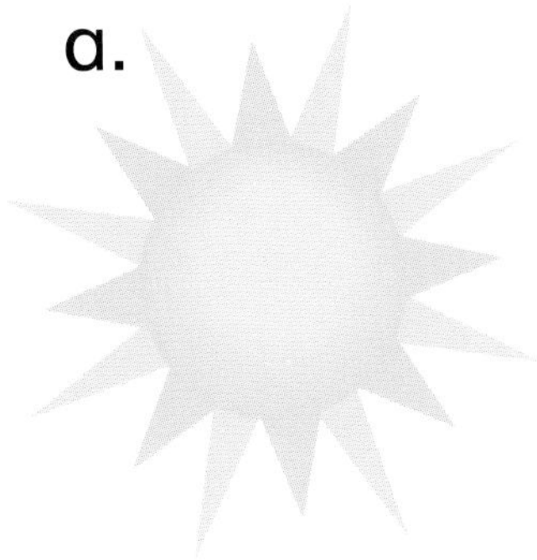

D 26-27 2. Some stars look small because they are
very _____ .

far away   close   dark

D 28-29 3. Long ago, people made up stories about
groups of _____ .

moons   stars   dots

D 30-31 4. Groups of stars that seem to form shapes
are called _____ .

animals   hunters   constellations

D 32-33 5. The moon has ____ light of its own.

much   some   no

D 34-35 6. Look at the pictures. Which picture shows things that are on the moon?

a.   b.    c.

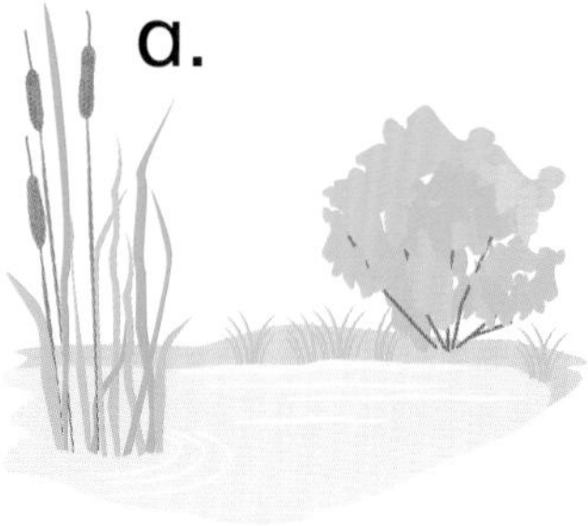

7. The moon has many holes called ____ .

craters   oceans   stars

D 36-37 8. The different shapes of the moon are called ____ .

craters   phases   circles

9. The moon moves around the ____ .

sun   earth   stars

Chapter 3 Looking at the Earth

D 42-43 1. You might dig through ____ when you dig in the earth.

sand   hot gases   craters

D 44-45 2. You can find soil, and water on ____ .

the stars   the sun   the earth

3. You can ____ rocks by color.

count   group   measure

D 46-47 **4.** You can find water, ____ , and bits of rock in soil.

    oceans   wind   air

D 48-49 **5.** Land is ____ the same everywhere on the earth.

    almost   not   always

D 50-51 **6.** Most of the water on earth is in ____ .

    rain   oceans   streams

7. Water on the ____ can be found in lakes, rivers, oceans, and streams.

    earth   moon   sun

D 52-53 **8.** People cannot drink ocean water because it is ____ .

    cold   warm   salty

D 54-55 **9.** Moving air is called ____ .

    space   wind   rain

10. Look at the pictures. Which picture shows what wind can do?

    a.   b. 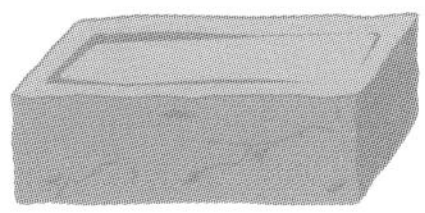   c.

Almost every day scientists learn new things about the world. They try to find the answers to problems. Scientists use scientific methods to help them with problems. They use steps in their methods. Sometimes scientists use the steps in different order. You can use these steps to find answers too.

Explain the Problem

Ask a question like this. Does sun heat air?

Make Observations

Tell about the size, the color, or the shape of things.

Give a Hypothesis

Try to answer the problem. Think of different ideas. Then do an experiment to test your ideas.

Make a Chart or Graph

Write what you learn in your chart or your graph.

Make Conclusions

Decide if your hypothesis is right or wrong.

Scientists are careful when they do experiments. You also need to be careful. Here are some safety rules to remember.

- Read each experiment carefully.

- Wear cover goggles when needed.

- Clean up spills right away.

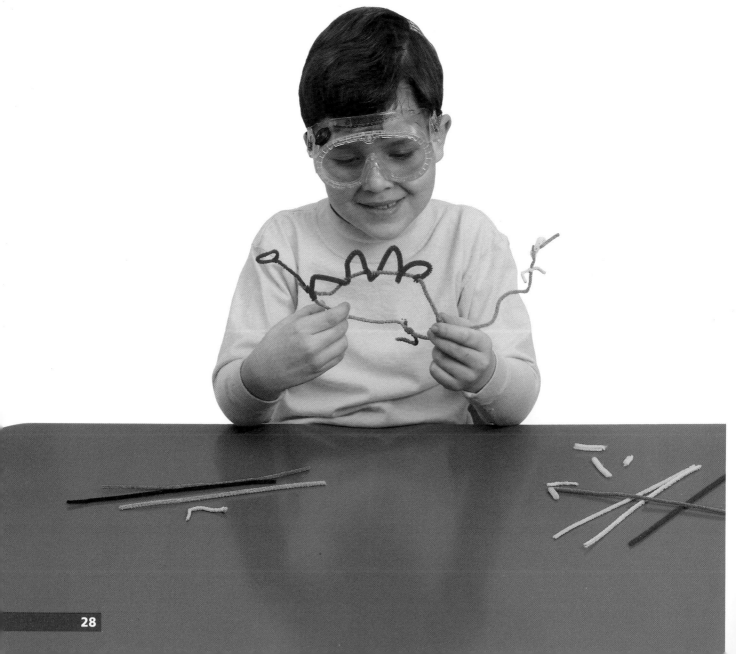

- Never taste or smell unknown things.

- Do not shine lights in someone's eyes.

- Clean up when you finish an experiment.

- Wash your hands after each experiment.

Experiment with Crickets

Sam catches a cricket in the basement. He knows that crickets eat apples. He wonders if a cricket might eat meat too.

Problem

Do crickets eat meat?

Give Your Hypothesis

Answer the problem.
Then do the experiment.

Follow the Directions

1 Make a chart like this one.

day	food that is left
1	
2	

2 Put the cricket in a box with air holes.

3 Give the cricket a bit of meat, a bit of apple, and some water.

4 Check the food each day for 2 days.

5 In your chart, write what food is left each day.

day 1	day 2

Tell Your Conclusion

Do crickets eat meat?

Experiment with Fossils

The museum has more fossils of bones and teeth than other parts of dinosaurs. Rosa wonders if hard parts make better fossils than softer parts.

Problem

Do hard objects make better fossils than soft objects do?

Give Your Hypothesis

Answer the problem.
Then do the experiment.

Follow the Directions

1 Make a chart like this one.

what I used to make the fossils	what the fossils looked like
shell	
cotton ball	

2 Fill 2 paper cups half full of clay.

3 Put a small shell on the clay in 1 cup.

4 Put a cotton ball on the clay in the other cup. Fill both cups with plaster of Paris.

5 Let the plaster harden. Pull the cup and clay away from the plaster.

6 In your chart, draw how the fossils look.

Tell Your Conclusion

Do hard objects make better fossils?

Experiment with Magnets

Mary spills paper clips on the table. David offers to help pick them up. Mary wants to use a magnet. David thinks two magnets will make the job easier.

Problem

Are two magnets stronger than one?

Give Your Hypothesis

Answer the problem.
Then do the experiment.

Follow the Directions

1 Make a chart like this one.

number of magnets	number of clips
1	
2	

2 Put paper clips on the table.

3 Use 1 magnet to pick up the paper clips. How many do you pick up? Write the number in the chart.

4 Use 2 magnets to pick up the clips. How many do you pick up? Write the number in your chart.

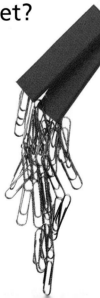

Tell Your Conclusion

Are 2 magnets stronger than 1 magnet?

Experiment with the Sun and Heat

Dan wants to swim. His mother says the water is too cold. She tells Dan to swim later when the water is warm. Dan wonders if the sun heats the water.

Problem

Can the sun heat water?

Give Your Hypothesis

Answer the problem.
Then do the experiment.

Follow the Directions

1 Make a chart like this one.

water	temperature
cup in sun	
cup in shade	

2 Fill 2 cups with cold water.

3 Put 1 cup in a sunny place. Put the other cup in a shady place.

4 Wait for 2 hours.

5 Measure the temperature of each cup.

6 Write the temperatures in your chart. Circle the cup that has warmer water.

Tell Your Conclusion

Can the sun heat water?

A **amphibian,** p. A49. a group of animals that lives on land and in water. Frogs and toads are amphibians.

antenna, p. A7. one of the feelers on the heads of insects. The butterfly used its antennas to smell flowers.

B **ball bearings,** p. C48. balls that turn freely so that work is made easier. Ball bearings help the wheels of a car spin.

battery, p. C34. something that stores electricity. Large batteries make cars start.

bird, p. A49. a group of animals with wings, feathers, and two legs. Most birds can fly.

bone, p. C52. hard part of the body. Bones move when muscles pull them.

C **cactus,** p. A16. a plant that grows in hot dry places. A cactus grows in the desert.

camouflage, A12. color or shape of an animal that matches the place where the animal lives. A chipmunk's camouflage makes it hard to see in the woods.

caterpillar, p. A10. an insect that looks like a furry or colorful worm. A fuzzy caterpillar crawled on a branch.

clay, p. D42. soil that is easily shaped when wet and hard when dry. Bricks are made from clay.

coal, p. D18. a black rock that gives off heat when it is burned. Coal comes from plants that died millions of years ago.

constellation, p. D30. a group of stars that form a pattern. The Big Dipper is a constellation.

crater, p. D34. a hole in the ground shaped like a bowl. The surface of the moon is covered with craters.

cricket, p. A32. an insect that makes noise by rubbing its wings together. The cricket chirped all night.

D **desert,** p. A16. a dry habitat that is usually sandy and without trees. It was sunny and hot in the desert.

dinosaur, p. B4. animal that lived millions of years ago. I read a book about dinosaurs.

diorama, p. B36. a scene that shows a group of animals and plants against a modeled background. Joey's diorama of the desert looked so real.

E **electricity,** p. C34. a kind of energy. Electricity makes the lights work.

endangered, p. B48. might become extinct. We should protect endangered animals.

energy, p. D16. the power to do work. Light, heat, and electricity are kinds of energy.

extinct, p. B44. no longer lives on the earth. Dinosaurs are extinct.

F **fish,** p. A49. a group of animals covered with scales that live in water. I like to watch the fish swimming in the tank.

float, p. A18. to be held up by air, water, or other liquid. A hot air balloon will float in the sky.

force, p. C7. something that makes something else move. A push is a force.

fossil, p. B24. a part or a print of a plant or animal that lived long ago. She studied the dinosaur fossil.

fuel, p. D18. anything you can burn that gives heat or power. Wood is a fuel.

G **gas,** p. D10. something that is not solid or liquid and has no shape of its own. The air we breathe is made of several gases.

globe, p. D33. a small, round copy of the earth. A globe has a map of the earth drawn on it.

group, p. A42. to gather a number of persons or things together. The teachers grouped all the second graders together.

H **habitat,** p. A26. a place where living things live. The bird has a nest habitat.

hatch, p. B34. to come out from an egg. Two chickens hatched today.

hibernate, p. A9. spend the winter resting or sleeping. Bears hibernate all winter.

I **insect,** p. A30. a small animal with six legs and three body parts. Bees are insects.

J **joint,** p. C52. the place in the body where two bones are joined. Your knee is a joint.

K **koala,** p. A36. a small gray animal that looks like a bear. Koalas live in Australia.

L **lever,** p. C46. a bar used for lifting They used a lever to lift a rock.

living, p. A44. having life; something that grows. Animals and plants are two kinds of living things.

lizard, p. B12. a long, reptile. The lizard ran over my foot.

M **machine,** p. C42. something that applies force to make work easier. My new bicycle is a machine.

magnet, p. C22. something that pulls pieces of metal to it. Nails will stick to a magnet.

mammal, p. A49. a group of animals usually covered with hair or fur. Cats are mammals.

model, p. A54. a small copy of something. A globe is a model of the earth.

moon, p. D32. the brightest thing in the night sky. Sunlight shining on the moon makes it shine.

muscle, p. C52. a part of the body that helps the body move. Leg muscles help you run.

N **nectar,** p. A6. sweet liquid found in flowers. Bees make nectar into honey.

nonliving, p. A44. something that does not have life. A book is a nonliving thing.

O **oil,** p. D18. a thick liquid that comes from under the ground. Oil is a fuel.

P **phases,** p. D37. the shapes of the lighted part of the moon. Michi drew the different phases of the moon.

plant, p. A47. any living thing that can make its own food from sunlight, air, and water. Trees are plants.

pole, p. C24. the end of a magnet. Magnets have north and south poles.

polluted, p. B50. made dirty and harmful. The children couldn't swim in the lake because the water was polluted.

pond, p. A28. water with land all around it. A pond is smaller than a lake.

protect, p. B54. to keep something safe. Mother birds protect their babies.

R **ramp,** p. C44. a slope that connects two levels. I pushed the box up the ramp.

reptile, p. A49. a group of animals with dry, rough skin. Snakes are reptiles.

rot, p. B26. become spoiled. The apples started to rot.

rough, p. C18. an uneven surface, not smooth. Sandpaper feels rough.

S **scale,** p. A50. the thin, hard pieces covering some fish, snakes and lizards. The scales on a fish are interesting.

scatter, p. A18. to throw a little bit here and there. The birds scattered the bird seed.

shell, p. B26. the hard, outside covering of some animals. Turtles have shells.

shelter, p. A30. something that covers something else from weather or danger. When it rained, everyone ran for shelter.

skeleton, p. B33. the bones of the body that support it and give it shape. You cannot see your skeleton.

smooth, p. C18. an even surface; not bumpy. The ice was so smooth that Bonnie was able to skate very fast.

soil, p. A27. dirt, the top layer of the earth. Marisa dug a small hole in the soil.

solar energy, p. D16. energy that comes from the sun. Many homes are heated with solar energy.

spider, p. A30. a very small animal with eight legs. I watched the spider spin its web.

star, p. D26. a tiny light in the night sky. A star is made up of hot, glowing gases.

stem, p. A14. the part of a plant that holds up leaves above the ground. The plant has a thin stem.

T **trunk,** p. A15. the main stem of a tree. The children leaned against the trunk of the big oak tree.

V **valley,** p D48. the low area between mountains or hills. Rivers often run through valleys.

W **web,** p. A56. a net of tiny threads made by a spider. The spider's sticky web helps it catch its food.

wheel, p. C43. a kind of machine. Wheels help make a skateboard move easily.

wildlife, p. A38. plants or animals not grown or tamed by people. It is a good idea to have parks for wildlife.

Acknowledgments

Outside Credits

Interior Design
Kym Abrams Design, Inc.
The Quarasan Group, Inc.
Rosa + Wesley Design Associates

Unless otherwise acknowledged, all photographs are the property of Scott, Foresman and Company. Page abbreviations are as follows: **(T) top, (C) center, (B) bottom, (L) left, (R) right, (INS) inset.**

Module A
Photographs
Front & Back Cover: Background: Patti Murray/EARTH SCENES Children's Photos: Michael Goss for Scott, Foresman and Company.

Page A2 John Shaw/Tom Stack & Associates **A3** Anna E.Zuckerman/Tom Stack & Associates **A5** Robert Lankinen/ The Wildlife Collection **A4(BL)** Don & Pat Valenti **A4(BR)** John Cancalosi/DRK Photo **A4-5(T)** Larry R.Ditto/Bruce Coleman, Inc. **A6** John Shaw/Tom Stack & Associates **A8-A9(T)** Jeff Foot/Bruce Coleman, Inc. **A8(B)** Mary Clay/ Tom Stack & Associates **A9(TR&B)** E.R.Degginger/ANIMALS ANIMALS **A12** Charlton Photographs **A13(T)** William E.Ferguson **A13(CL)** E.R.Degginger **A13(CR)** Marcia W.Griffen/ ANIMALS ANIMALS **A13(B)** Michael Fogden/DRK Photo **A14** Robert Frerck/Tony Stone Worldwide **A16** James Tallon **A18** David Cavagnaro/ Peter Arnold, Inc. **A24(L)** Tom Bean/DRK Photo **A24-A25(T)** Tom Bean/DRK Photo **A24-A25(B)** Margot Granitsas/The Image Works **A25(T)** Cameramann International Ltd. **A25(B)** Tom Bean/DRK Photo **A26-A27** Anna E.Zuckermann/Tom Stack & Associates **A28(T)** George I.Bernard/ANIMALS ANIMALS **A28(C)** Ray Richardson/ANIMALS ANIMALS **A28(B)** Ralph A.Reinhold/ANIMALS ANIMALS **A29(T)** Patti Murray/ANIMALS ANIMALS **A29(B)** E.R.Degginger **A34(T)** Rudi VonBriel **A34(B)-A35(B)** Esao Hashimoto/ANIMALS ANIMALS **A35(TL)** Ron Austing/Photo Researchers, Inc. **A36** Brian Parker/Tom Stack & Associates **A46(TL)** Aaron Haupt/David Frazier Photolibrary **A46(TR)** Stephen J.Krasemann/DRK Photo **A46(B)** Robert A.Tyrell/Oxford Scientific Films/ANIMALS ANIMALS **A47** John D.Cunningham/Visuals Unlimited **A50** Van Welsen/Tony Stone Worldwide **A52** David M.Dennis/Tom Stack & Associates **A53(TL)** E.R.Degginger **A53(R)** Hans Pfletschinger/Peter Arnold, Inc.

Illustrations
Page A7 Laurie O'Keefe **A15** Cindy Brodie **A20-21** Don Charles Meighan **A30-31** Erika Kors **A38-39** Nancy Lee Walter **A44-45** Renee Daily **A48-49** Kim Mulkey **A56-57** Don Charles Meighan **A61** Mike Eagle

Module B
Photographs
Front & Back Cover: Children's Photos: Michael Goss for Scott, Foresman and Company.

Page B2(T) Alex Kerstitch/Visuals Unlimited **B2(C)** Kjell B.Sandved/Visuals Unlimited **B20-B21(T) & B20(B)** Bruce Selyem/Museum of the Rockies, Montana State University **B21(TR)** Scott Berner/Visuals Unlimited **B21(C)** British Museum of Natural History **B21(BR)** Bruce Selyem/Museum of The Rockies, Montana State University **B26** William E.Ferguson **B27(T)** Alex Kerstitch/ Visuals Unlimited **B27(B)** Kjell B.Sandved/Visuals Unlimited **B28** Phil Degginger **B32** American Museum of Natural History, New York City Neg.2143 **B48(T)** Wendy Smith/Bob Rozinski/Tom Stack & Associates **B48(B)** Marty Stouffer/ ANIMALS ANIMALS **B49(TL)** Kerry T.Givens/Tom Stack & Associates **B49(TR)** William E.Ferguson **B49(B)** Gerald & Buff Corsi/Tom Stack & Associates **B56-B57** Gregory G.Dimijian, M.D./Photo Researchers, Inc. **B60** David R.Austen/Stock Boston

Illustrations
Page B2 Raymond E. Smith **B4-5** Robert Masheris **B6-7** Raymond E. Smith **B10** Ka Botzis **B12-13** Robert Masheris **B14-15** Cecile Duray-Bito **B16-17** Cecile Duray-Bito **B22** Ka Botzis **B30-31** Cecile Duray-Bito **B34-35** Ka Botzis **B36-37** Raymond E. Smith **B38-39** Sharron O'Neil **B42-43** Ronald C. Lipking **B44-45** Roberta Polfus **B46-47** Edward Brooks **B52** Rondi Collette **B61** Mike Eagle

Module C
Photographs
Front & Back Cover: Background: Holt Confer/DRK Photo Children's Photographs: Michael Goss for Scott, Foresman and Company.

Page C2(B) William E.Ferguson **C42** William E.Ferguson **C46** E.R.Degginger **C60** Courtesy, Huffy Bicycles

Illustrations
Page C4-5 Rondi Collette **C8-9** Yvette Banek **C18-19** Linda Hawkins **C28-29** Meryl Henderson **C36-37** Lisa Pompelli **C40-41** Cindy Brodie **C52-53** Vincent Perez **C57** Vincent Perez **C61** Mike Eagle

Module D
Photographs
Front & Back Cover: Background: E.R.Degginger   Children's Photos: Michael Goss for Scott, Foresman and Company.

Page D3(B) Tom Bean/DRK Photo   **D4-D5** Joseph A.DiChello
D6-D7(T) Lawrence Migdale/Stock Boston
D6-D7(B) Mike J.Howell/Stock Boston   **D10** NASA
D16 Bob Daemmrich/Stock Boston   **D26-D27** Dennis DiCicco
D32 E.R.Degginger   **D34** NASA   **D36-D37** Dennis DiCicco
D48 Stephen J.Krasemann/DRK Photo   **D49** Tom Bean/DRK Photo
D50-D51(T) Telegraph Colour Library/FPG
D50-D51(B) Larry Ulrich/DRK Photo
D51(TR) Scott Berner/Visuals Unlimited
D51(BR) Stan Osolinski/Tony Stone Worldwide
D60 Alan Carey/The Image Works

Illustrations
Page D3 Pam Hohman   **D14-15** Rondi Collette
D18-19 Raymond E. Smith   **D20-21** Lisa Pompelli
D24-25 Diana Philbrook   **D28-29** Pam Hohman
D38-39 Nan Brooks   **D56-57** Linda Hawkins
D61 Mike Eagle

Back Matter
Photographs
Page 9 Bob Daemmrich/The Image Works
Illustrations
Pages 10-25, 38-46 Precision Graphics